14 Sacred Solos

High Voice

Edited by Richard Walters

To access companion recorded performances
and accompaniments online, visit:
www.halleonard.com/mylibrary

Enter Code
5743-8601-9708-4632

Singers on the Recordings:
*Tanya Kruse, soprano; **Steven Stolen, tenor; ***Stuart Mitchell, tenor

Pianists on the Recordings:
+Catherine Bringerud (Performances only); Richard Walters for all remaining tracks

ISBN 978-0-634-08137-8

HAL•LEONARD®
CORPORATION
7777 W. BLUEMOUND RD. P.O. BOX 13819 MILWAUKEE, WI 53213

In Australia Contact:
Hal Leonard Australia Pty. Ltd.
4 Lentara Court
Cheltenham, Victoria, 3192 Australia
Email: ausadmin@halleonard.com.au

Visit Hal Leonard Online at
www.halleonard.com

for Sharon

Ah, Holy Jesus

Johann Heermann, 1630
translated by Robert S. Bridges, 1899

"Herzliebster Jesu"
Johann Crüger, 1640
arranged by Richard Walters

guil - ty? Who brought this up - on thee? A - las, my trea - son, Je - sus, hath un -

done thee! 'Twas I, Lord Je - sus, I it was de - nied thee,

I cru - ci - fied thee. For me, kind Je - sus,

was thy in - car - na - tion, Thy mor - tal sor - row, and thy life's ob - la - tion;

Brother James' Air

Based on Psalm 23

James L. Bain
(1840-1925)
arranged by Brian Dean

lead - eth me, the qui - et wa - ters by.

bless - ed - ness E'en for His own name's

2. My sake.

Yea, tho I walk through

shad-owed vale, yet will I fear no ill, For Thou art with me

Amazing Grace

John Newton (1725-1807)

Early American Folk Melody
arranged by Richard Walters

fear, And grace my fears re - lieved; _____ How prec - ious _____

did that grace _____ ap - pear The _____ hour I _____ first be - lieved. _____

3. The Lord has _____ prom - ised good to

me His word my _____ hope se - cures; He will _____ my _____

*The singer is encouraged to embellish the melody; small notes are stylistic suggestions.

shield and por - tion __ be as __ long as __ life en -

decresc.

dures. __

mp

p

pp

4. Through

man - y __ dan - gers toils and snares I have al -

mp

read - y come; __ 'Tis grace __ hath __ brought me

8va

8va

safe ___ thus _ far, And grace will _ lead me home. ___

5. Yea, when this ___

flesh and heart shall fail, And mor - tal ___ life shall

cease, ___ I shall ___ po - sess with - in ___ the ___

veil, a life of __ joy and peace. _____ 6. When

More Broadly

we've been __ there ten thou - sand __ years, bright shin - ing __ as the

sun, _____ We've no __ less __ days to sing __ God's __ praise __

Than _____ when _____ we first be

gun. _____

Was blind _____ but now I see. _____

* A third vocal line option:

Than ___ when _____ we first be - gun. _____

Ave Maria

Franz Schubert

A - ve Ma - ri - -
A - ve Ma - ri - -

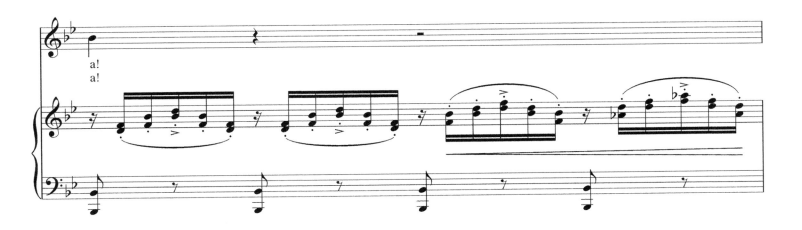

a!
a!

sim.

dim.

Balm in Gilead

Jeremiah 8 : 22

African-American Spiritual
arranged by Harry T. Burleigh

There __ is a

Balm in Gil - e - ad, To make the wound - ed

whole ___ There __ is a Balm in Gil - e - ad, to

make the wound - ed whole ___ There ___ is a Balm in Gil - e - ad, To heal the sin - sick soul. If you can preach like Pe - ter, if you can pray like Paul, Go home and tell your neigh - bor, "He

rit.

a tempo

decresc.

The Call

George Herbert

Ralph Vaughan Williams

Deep River

African-American Spiritual
arranged by Harry T. Burleigh

camp - ground. Deep _____ riv - er, my home is o - ver Jor - dan _____ Deep _____ riv - er, Lord, I want to cross o - ver in - to camp - ground. Oh, don't you want _ to go _____ to that

How Can I Keep from Singing

American Folksong
Arranged by Richard Walters

Allegretto; steady

to that rock I'm cling-ing. __ It sounds an ech - o __ in my soul. How

can I keep from sing-ing?__ 2. What though the tem - pest round me rears, I

know the truth, it liv-eth. __ What though the dark - ness round me close, Songs

in the night it giv-eth. __ No storm can shake my in-most calm while

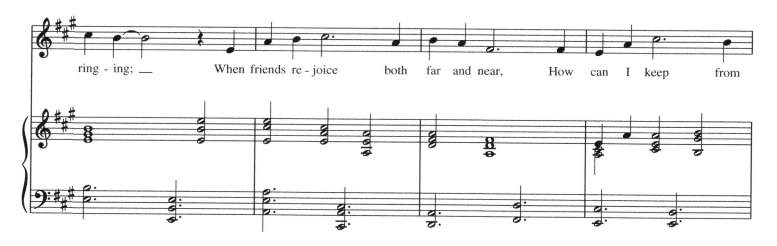

ring - ing; ___ When friends re - joice both far and near, How can I keep from

sing - ing? ___ In pris - on cell and dun - geon vile Our thoughts to them are

wing - ing. ___ When friends by shame are ___ un - de - filed, How can I keep from

Jesu, Joy of Man's Desiring

Johann Sebastian Bach
Arranged by John Reed

Because of length, a singer may choose to perform just verse one. This has been the case on the companion CD.

light.
springs.

Word of God, our flesh _____ that fash - ion'd
Theirs is beau - ty's fair - est plea - sure,

mf

With the fire of
Theirs is wis - dom's

p   cresc.

life _____ im - pas - sion'd.
ho - liest trea - sure.

Striv - ing still to
Thou dost ev - er

Truth un - known,
lead Thine own,

Soar - ing, dy - ing, round ____ Thy ____
In the love of joys ____ un -

throne.
known.

Sheep May Safely Graze

from Cantata No. 208

Johann Sebastian Bach
adapted by Christopher Ruck

If the piece feels too long for your church service purpose, two options may be employed:
end at the "Fine" before proceeding to the "B" section; or rather than "D.S. al Fine" at the end of "B,"
repeat back just to the last four bars before "Fine". The recording repeats back to the 𝄋.

Last time

Fine

1st time

He who rules with vi - sion guid - ing ___

Brings us ___ rest and peace a - bid - ing, ___

Saves our souls from ___ end - less ___ night.

He who ___

rules with vi - sion ____ guid - ing, ___ Brings us ___

rest and peace a - bid - ing, Rest

and peace, Rest

and peace a - bid - ing,

D.S. al Fine

Saves our souls from end - less night.

Just a Closer Walk with Thee

Traditional American Song
arranged by Richard Walters

We Are Climbing Jacob's Ladder

African-American Spiritual
arranged by Richard Walters

1. We are climb - ing Ja - cob's lad - der we are

climb - ing Ja - cob's lad - der, we are climb - ing

Ja - cob's lad - der, sol - diers of the cross.

Espressivo, rubato

3. Do you think I'll make a good sol- dier? Do you think I'll make a good sol- dier? Do you think I'll make a Chris- tian sol- dier sol- dier of the cross?

Poco più mosso

mf

4. Rise, shine, give God your glo - ry, Rise,

with pedal

shine, give God your glo - ry, _____ rise, shine, _

f

f *rhythmically*

give God your glo - ry, sol - diers of the cross. _____

8va

f *rhythmically*

decresc.

mp

We are climb-ing Ja-cob's lad-der, we are climb-ing Ja-cob's lad-der, we are climb-ing Ja-cob's lad-der, sol-diers of the cross.

sub. *p*

(*p*)

8va

Wondrous Love

American Folk Hymn
arranged by Richard Walters

bliss To bear the dread - ful curse for my

soul, for my soul, To bear the dread - ful curse for my

a little faster ♩ = 96

soul.

mp

Wayfaring Stranger

Southern American Folksong
arranged by Richard Walters

This song seems like a spiritual, and it may well be one, but those origins have been unconfirmed.

roam. I'm on-ly go - in' o - ver Jor - dan, I'm on-ly

go - in' o - ver home.

2. I know dark clouds _____ will gath - er 'round me. I know my

way _____ is rough and steep, but gol - den fields _____ lie out be -

fore me _____ where God's re - deemed _____ shall ev - er sleep. I'm go - in'

there _____ to see my moth - er. She said she'd meet _____ me when I

come. I'm on - ly go - in' o - ver Jor - dan. I'm on - ly

go - in' o - ver home.